AGES OF INITIATION

Ages of Initiation

The First Two Christian Millennia

With CD-ROM of Source Excerpts

Paul Turner

A Liturgical Press Book

THE LITURGICAL PRESS
Collegeville, Minnesota

www.litpress.org

Cover design by Greg Becker.

1   2   3   4   5   6   7

Library of Congress Cataloging-in-Publication Data

Turner, Paul, 1953–
    Ages of initiation : the first two Christian millennia : with CD-ROM of source excerpts / Paul Turner.
        p.   cm.
    Includes bibliographical references.
    ISBN 0-8146-2711-0 (alk. paper)
    1. Initiation rites—Admission age—Religious aspects—Catholic Church—History of doctrines.   I. Title.

BX2045.I553 T87   2000
264'.02081'09—dc21   00-042846

Dedication

MARGARETÆ BERTRANDÆ S.S.N.D. SODALI QVÆ
DISCIPVLOS DESIDERIO DISCENDI PROPRIO CONFIRMAVIT
COMMVNITATEM SORORVM DVXIT IN FIDE PRIMVM
FAMILIAM SVAM AMAVIT PER OMNES ÆTATES
ATQVE AVCTOREM MYSTERIIS HISTORIÆ INITIAVIT
DEDICATVR HÆC PROLATORVM DISPVTANDORVMQVE SEQVENTIA

Contents

Acknowledgments   viii

Introduction   ix

Chapter One: The New Testament Church (1–100)   1

Chapter Two: Emerging Ritual Patterns (101–300)   4

Chapter Three: The Golden Age (301–500)   7

Chapter Four: Liturgical Development (501–700)   12

Chapter Five: The Era of Charlemagne (701–828)   16

Chapter Six: Regulating Initiation (829–964)   20

Chapter Seven: Pastoral Concerns (965–1214)   24

Chapter Eight: The Age of Discretion (1215–1519)   28

Chapter Nine: Reformation (1520–1592)   34

Chapter Ten: The Ritualization of First Communion (1593–1773)   37

Chapter Eleven: Sequence (1774–1909)   41

Chapter Twelve: The Diversification of Tradition (1910–2000)   45

Conclusions   49

How to Use the CD-ROM   70

Acknowledgments

I wish to thank

Conception Abbey Library; Rockhurst College Library; The Department of Special Collections, Hesburgh Library, University of Notre Dame, which remembered;

Rita Ferrone, Rick Janet, Michael Witczak, Michael Driscoll, George Smiga, and Maxwell Johnson, who read;

Brother Thomas Sullivan, o.s.b., who located;

Thom Morris, who encouraged;

The people of St. Regis Parish, who supported;

My family and friends, who waited;

God, who loves people and time.

—P.T.

Introduction

The age of a confirmation candidate varies considerably from house to house. In some circumstances First Communion precedes confirmation; in others it follows. Bishops, pastors, and catechists set policies for age and sequence based on their understanding of the significance of these Catholic sacraments. Parents often wonder why the policies change.

Those who set sacramental policies generally turn to the Church's history to support their decisions. But historical summaries often overlook the nuances in shifting patterns of tradition. Consequently, some decisions are made on incomplete information.

This history documents the age of candidates for baptism, confirmation, and the first reception of Communion in the Catholic Church, and the sequence in which a person received these sacraments. It tracks the circumstances that caused patterns to form and shift. Its purpose is to enlighten those who form sacramental policies as well as those who live by them.

Today many circumstances affect the age and sequence for baptism, confirmation, and First Communion. Catechumens, who range in age from school children to seniors, celebrate baptism, then confirmation, and then Eucharist in the same ceremony. But children born of Catholic parents may be baptized as infants and celebrate confirmation and Eucharist in different ceremonies over a period of eighteen years or more; in many cases their confirmation follows the first reception of Communion. Still, the Church today calls these three rites "sacraments of initiation."

The phrase poses problems since it was popularized only in the last century due to work in the field of anthropology. Human beings have always incorporated rites of initiation into their societies, as evidenced by ancient cultures like Egypt and Greece, contemporary tribal ritual, and in groups as commonplace as scouting and benevolent associations.

To join a group, one participates in some ritual. But societies have not always termed these rituals "initiation rites."

Nor is it clear to which rites the phrase applies. At its simplest level it refers to those rites by which a person joins a particular body. However, some apply the phrase by analogy to rites that accompany advancement from one stage to another within the same body.

Consequently, even though baptism, confirmation, and First Communion are termed "sacraments of initiation" today, the terminology is new whereas the rites are old. Furthermore, in the past the Western church did not always consistently recognize confirmation and First Communion as initiation rites, and the age, occasion, and sequence of their reception varied considerably. At first, when new members were primarily converts from non-Christian communities, a single celebration of these ceremonies concluded their catechetical formation. Later, when new members were primarily infants born within the stabilized Christian assembly, the rites of initiation diffused into distinct ceremonies celebrated over a span of years in one's life. Ecclesial, pastoral, doctrinal, and catechetical reasons caused the changes in the recipient's age. Moreover, once confirmation and the first reception of Communion became detached from their original context, their sequence depended on external considerations more than on their internal meaning.

Today, more than any other time in history, opinions abound about the appropriate age of candidates for these sacraments and the sequence of their reception. Tension arises between the expectation of catechetical preparation and the proclamation of God's free gift of grace. If confirmation and First Communion are sacraments of initiation, why should they not be offered as freely as infant baptism? If they are treasures reserved for a more mature Christian, why call them initiation? The determination of the appropriate age for these sacraments will depend upon the relationship between human maturity and the sacramental encounter with God. The determination of their sequence will depend upon their meaning as independent rituals and in relationship with each other.

This book summarizes the full text on the CD, which divides the twenty centuries of Christianity into twelve chapters. Each chapter subdivides into units that pair introductory material with a collection of citations, and then concludes with a bulleted summary. Translations are the author's, except where noted in the bibliography. The reader who wishes to consult original references will find direction in the bibliography; the entry for each primary source includes the pagination generally reserved for footnotes. The collection of sources does not pretend to be exhaustive; it does aspire to fairly represent the periods under study.

Chapter One

The New Testament Church

1–100

The good news of the resurrection turned the hearts of many to the teaching of Jesus of Nazareth. Baptism ritualized their conversion and Eucharist celebrated their belief.

The books of the New Testament, composed in the second half of the first century, leave some indications of the early practice of initiation.

This chapter examines the baptisms of the apostolic church and the life and ministry of Jesus that may have influenced their form. Other New Testament passages shed light on the baptismal ceremony and the age of candidates. The Scriptures also introduce the Eucharist of the apostolic church, the life and ministry of Jesus that influenced it, and data that suggest the age of and criteria for participation.

The New Testament records only a simple ceremony for baptism in the apostolic church.

Baptisms in the New Testament are recorded as simple ceremonies. Whether the group was large or small, whether indoors or out, a small amount of catechesis was given and the ritual required only a confession of sins, a profession of faith, and the pouring of water by a minister of the community. Some catechesis may have followed baptism, as did participation in the community's life.

1

The form of baptism in the apostolic church was probably influenced by the baptism of Jesus and the baptizing ministry of his disciples.

The baptism of Jesus served as a turning point in his own ministry. He incorporated baptism into the ministry of his followers. The practice probably influenced the development of baptism as a post-resurrection ceremony for new Christians. The baptisms of John and within the ministry of Jesus, while not the same as Christian baptism that followed the resurrection, implied an adult capacity for repentance.

The New Testament suggests a formula for the words of baptism, the abundant use of water, and a minister.

Baptism remained a simple ritual in the New Testament, but certain elements could already be identified. A formula for the words of baptism appears at the end of Matthew's gospel. The narratives concerning baptism and the commentary on the ritual in the epistles all assume an abundant use of water. A minister always played a role. One did not baptize himself or herself.

The apostolic church either employed or inspired anointing, handlaying, and clothing in baptisms.

To express the meaning of baptism, the New Testament used images of anointing, handlaying, and clothing. It is doubtful that any of these were used regularly with baptisms, but the appearance of these images in sacred texts led to their inclusion in later baptismal rituals.

The New Testament neither proves nor excludes the possibility that infants were baptized, but it is reasonable to assume that they were.

There are no clear accounts of infant baptism in the New Testament, but the circumstances do not exclude the possibility. There are records of household baptisms, for example, and Paul compared baptism to the (infant) rite of circumcision. Jesus' ministry to children formed part of his mission to the needy.

The New Testament never describes a baptismal Eucharist, but the Eucharist was shared in the community of the baptized.

None of the ceremonies of baptism described in the New Testament includes a Eucharist. The Eucharist was shared only among the baptized, but there is no evidence that Communion was included in the baptismal rituals of the apostolic church.

The traditions of and about the Eucharist reported in the gospels probably influenced the form of the Eucharist in the apostolic church.

As the baptismal ministry of Jesus influenced the form of baptism in the apostolic church, so the Last Supper and the biblical traditions about the breaking of the bread influenced the shape of the Eucharist of the apostolic church.

Paul expected appropriate behaviors by those participating in the Eucharist.

Although baptism served as a gateway to participating in the Eucharist, Paul expected those sharing the sacred meal to demonstrate appropriate behavior.

The New Testament neither affirms nor denies the reception of Communion by children.

There is no evidence about children being excluded from or included in the Eucharist. If they were baptized, which seems likely though not demonstrable, it seems reasonable to assume that they also shared the Eucharist.

Chapter Two

Emerging Ritual Patterns

101–300

Ritual patterns of baptismal initiation began to emerge in the post-apostolic Church. Baptism, anointing with oil, handlaying, and Communion all appeared as ritual elements of initiation by the end of the third century. The Church welcomed candidates of all ages, including infants. But the sequence of the rites depended on the local community's preference and the health of the candidate. Christianity was spreading throughout many different centers of civilization, cosmopolitan cities known for their wealth and rich traditions. They each developed variations in the patterns of initiation.

The first baptismal rituals of the second century followed the New Testament example of simplicity.

The earliest record of a baptismal liturgy followed the pattern of the New Testament. It appears that baptism took place as an independent ritual, not connected with other ceremonies like handlaying and Eucharist.

Eucharist was reserved for the baptized.

In keeping with the New Testament tradition, only the baptized participated in the Eucharist. This expectation is well attested in various places of the Christian world.

4

Eucharist became part of the baptismal liturgy.

The first clear reference to sharing the Eucharist at a baptismal liturgy comes from the work of Justin the Martyr (+165). Everyone present for the baptism took part in Communion; no other factor (e.g., one's age) was mentioned. Although this single text does indicate Eucharist at a baptismal liturgy, the silence of other sources suggests that a baptismal Eucharist was not yet widely practiced.

People joined Jesus' two promises of eternal life: for those born of water and the Spirit and for those who ate the bread of life.

Two sayings of Jesus in John's Gospel (3:5 and 6:53) began to be connected. They promised eternal life for those who believed and were baptized and for those who ate and drank the body and blood of Christ.

In Syria an anointing preceded baptism; this anointing signified that of the Messiah, priest and king, the consecration of the candidate for the Eucharist, physical and spiritual healing, forgiveness, and power.

In Syria, and possibly in Egypt, a ritual anointing with handlaying preceded baptism. The meaning of this anointing was interpreted in different ways.

In North Africa Tertullian's anointing followed baptism, with priestly and messianic symbolism.

At the same time as these developments in Syria, another tradition arose placing anointing after baptism, as evidenced in the writings of Tertullian from North Africa. He assigned the anointing a christological significance.

In Rome two anointings followed baptism: one by a presbyter in the name of Jesus, the second with the imposition of the bishop's hand and a prayer for the gift of the Holy Spirit.

The *Apostolic Tradition* describes two anointings after baptism—as well as one before. It may represent a conflation of the emergent patterns.

The Apostolic Tradition *describes an elaborate baptismal Eucharist.*

The baptismal Eucharist in the *Apostolic Tradition* invited the newly baptized to approach several ministers at successive stations for the body of Christ, a cup of water, a cup of milk and honey, as well as the blood of Christ.

The Church affiliated baptism with sacred days, the needs of the sick, and the birth of children.

The Church began to associate baptism with certain days. Tertullian preferred Easter and the season up to Pentecost, but these times were not universally endorsed. The sick could be baptized at any time, and some infants were baptized shortly after birth.

In case of grave illness, baptism was conferred, even without the customary minister, time, and place.

Although it was becoming the custom for baptism to take place by a bishop at a designated time of year in a sacred place, an illness of the one to be baptized could cause exceptions. Many were baptized by other ministers, apart from the preferred times, in diverse locations.

Infants were baptized.

The practice of infant baptism is well attested in the second and third centuries, though not everyone agreed with the custom. Some were probably baptized shortly after birth if their health appeared unstable. Others were baptized with adults.

Infants received Communion.

Many infants received Communion at their baptism and throughout their infancy, according to several documents of the period.

Chapter Three

The Golden Age

301–500

By the fourth century initiates of all ages generally celebrated baptism, anointing, and Communion in the same ceremony. Characterized by ample ritual gestures and beautifully crafted prayers, the initiation rites entered a golden age, presenting the drama of the paschal mystery alive within the community of believers. However, even as the full formal rites crystallized, extraordinary pastoral needs were already causing the occasional celebration of baptism alone and the deferral of the other rites.

During this period Christianity became established as the official religion of the Roman Empire. The expansion of the Church produced the need for councils, the theological reflection of Church Fathers, and the further diversification of ministerial roles. As Christianity became official, it needed to define orthodoxy in clearer ways than before.

Divergent initiatory patterns became more similar; e.g., the Syrian sequence, which placed anointing before baptism, changed to resemble the rest of the Christian world. But the occasions for initiation remained diverse, both in its full and simpler forms.

At first, Syrian initiation rites placed anointing before baptism.

Evidence from Syria during this period suggests that the churches there kept the anointing before baptism, as a protective seal for the one renouncing Satan. This practice had already developed in the previous century. The same pattern may have perdured into the fourth century in Egypt as well.

7

By the end of the fourth century, Syrian initiation rites added an anointing between baptism and Eucharist.

Probably due to the influence of the rest of the Christian world, the Syrian rites began to include an anointing between baptism and Eucharist. Ministers did not move the pre-baptismal anointing to a later position in the rite; rather, they added another anointing. The Council of Laodicea (381?) may have induced the change.

Virtually the whole Church, then, celebrated the initiation rites in the sequence baptism-anointing-Eucharist.

The principal rites of initiation followed a similar pattern throughout the Church: baptism, then anointing and/or handlaying, and Eucharist. Other rites, for example a pre-baptismal anointing, continued to develop.

Ambrose incorporated a post-baptismal anointing, a signing of the forehead, and a prayer for the coming of the Holy Spirit under the form of seven gifts—signs that Christ had "confirmed" the neophyte.

Ambrose describes a rite after baptism that included an anointing, signation of the forehead, and prayer for the coming of the Holy Spirit. He says this showed that Christ had "confirmed" or "strengthened" the neophyte. The post-baptismal anointing was still not called "confirmation." Ambrose was the first to attribute to the anointing the function of strengthening. His prayer for the sevenfold gift of the Holy Spirit gained widespread use in post-baptismal rites.

Since only the baptized participated in the Eucharist, the baptismal Eucharist took on greater significance in initiation.

The baptismal Eucharist, virtually absent among the documents from the first two centuries of Christianity, attained customary usage by the fourth century. Documents from most areas of the fourth- and fifth-century Christian world widely affirm the baptism of neophytes in the context of a Eucharist.

Easter became the preferred date for baptism, but certain areas developed their own customary days.

Because of the connection between the resurrection of Christ and the sacramental meaning of baptism, Easter became the preferred date for baptisms. Exceptions existed, and some areas developed different days or multiple feasts for baptism throughout the year.

In emergency, baptism could be administered at any time.

Since the unpredictable health of infants and catechumens remained an abiding problem, baptism could be administered at any time if the faithful feared the death of a baptismal candidate. Thus, although there were preferred liturgical dates for baptizing, pastoral exceptions abounded.

Theologians defended the custom of baptizing infants.

The practice of baptizing infants continued to provoke some discussion and debate. Several theologians defended the practice based on beliefs that children modeled baptismal innocence and shared equally in the grace of redemption.

The Church came to believe that the baptism of infants cleansed them from original sin.

The concept of original sin began to play an important part in the defense of infant baptism. The Church believed that baptism cleansed from sin. However, infants were incapable of personal sin. They had to be cleansed from some other sin, one for which they held no responsibility. The result of baptism began to be expressed in this way: that it cleansed from original sin. Because of Augustine's stature among theologians, his writings influenced the Church's belief on this point for generations.

Some infants were baptized at birth, others some days or years later, and others after they had grown to adulthood.

Even though the baptism of infants was common, the occasions diversified. Testimony from the fourth and fifth centuries indicates some variation in the age of a child at baptism. Some were baptized at birth, but others received baptism days, years, or even decades later.

In an emergency, baptism could be administered apart from Easter, away from the cathedral, and by a minister other than the bishop.

The baptism of candidates with questionable health could take place at a different time of year, apart from Easter. The other circumstances of baptism could also change to accommodate the pastoral need.

Infants continued to receive Communion.

As in the previous centuries, the Communion of infants is well attested throughout this period. Since the Eucharist had been linked to the baptismal ceremony, even infants participated in this Communion at their baptism and during their lives.

When someone other than a bishop baptized—due to illness, distance from the cathedral, or heresy—the baptized who were able went to the bishop later to receive the omitted rites.

By the beginning of the fourth century the rites of initiation began to split. For the first time, considerable concern arose about those baptized in emergency situations who did not receive the other parts of the initiation rites. Such circumstances included the sick and those who lived a distance from the cathedral. Those whose condition changed after such an emergency baptism were asked to present themselves to the bishop for his part of the rite. There is no evidence that the Eucharist was deferred for those baptized by a minister other than the bishop.

Persons baptized by someone who was not a bishop were still considered saved if they died before seeing him.

The recognition that some people in special circumstances were being baptized in emergencies raised the question about the effects of their baptism. The leaders of the Church assured the faithful that if anyone died after baptism but before going to the bishop, he or she was still considered saved.

Some presbyters and deacons administered complete initiation rites, but bishops generally preferred to reserve the anointing for themselves.

By the fifth century legislation appeared restricting the ministry of post-baptismal anointing to bishops. Presbyters and deacons must have been performing this ritual themselves, thus provoking the bishops to enact more restrictive legislation.

The term "confirmation" named the chrismation by a bishop after baptism and handlaying in the reconciliation of heretics.

There were three circumstances that called for a post-baptismal rite led by the bishop: the baptism by another minister of a person feared to be near death, the baptism by another minister of a person who lived a distance from the cathedral, and the baptism of someone in a heretical sect. When any of the persons in these circumstances approached the bishop, the rite he performed for them came to be called "confirmation." Gallic usage applied the term to those baptized in orthodox Christianity. Roman usage applied it to those baptized by heretics. The rite was not called "initiation," and there is no clear evidence from this period that the handlaying and anointing performed by a bishop during a baptismal ceremony at the cathedral was called "confirmation." Confirmation, as the term was first used, probably meant a rite performed by a bishop some time after a baptism performed by someone else. It "confirmed" or "affirmed" the baptism.

Participation in the Eucharist probably continued for those baptized without the bishop's chrismation.

There is no evidence that the Eucharist was deferred from baptism when someone other than the bishop performed the ceremony. It appears that the intimate connection of baptism and Eucharist remained unbroken at this time. Hence, someone baptized by a minister other than the bishop received Communion before confirmation.

Chapter Four

Liturgical Development

501–700

Throughout the sixth and seventh centuries the liturgical texts and ministerial roles of initiation developed. Politically, the decline and fall of the Western empire increased the authority of the papacy and the significance of monasticism; liturgically, it also permitted regional variations in sacramental practice. Tensions over uniformity in ritual and authority in ministry affected the development of the initiation rites.

The basic initiatory complex remained the same: baptism, anointing, and Eucharist at the same ceremony. However, the number of baptisms taking place when no bishop could be present increased; confirmation and the bishop's role in it became more significant. Furthermore, when the anointing was deferred from baptism, baptismal Communion remained in place; the sequence of rites effectively altered in those cases to baptism, Eucharist, anointing—but at two different occasions separated by some time. In these circumstances confirmation was still not termed a "rite of initiation."

During this period the conventional initiatory pattern from the preceding centuries endured, along with the double criteria for establishing the occasion for initiation: either a fixed liturgical day, or a day pertaining to the candidate's birth or ill-health. People started to think about maturity in terms of age, but baptism, confirmation, and Communion remained open to infants. Confirmation developed a theology and suffered widespread disagreement about the necessity of its celebration and the minister of anointing.

When a bishop was present, the conventional sequence of initiation rites was baptism, anointing, Communion.

During this period liturgical texts were written in more detail. Those describing the baptismal rites for bishops preserved the now-conventional sequence of rites: baptism, anointing, and Communion. This anointing began to be called "confirmation," a term borrowed from the anointing that the bishop administered in cases where he was not the minister of baptism. Written liturgical texts were composed primarily for bishops, not for other ministers, but the number of baptisms bishops actually performed probably continued to decline.

Easter and Pentecost remained the preferred days for baptism, although any day sufficed for emergencies.

The Church retained in theory the preference for Easter and Pentecost as baptismal days. However, any day was permitted in case of necessity, and concern over the infant mortality rate caused the Church tacitly to approve baptism on any day shortly after birth. However, the preference for Easter and Pentecost remained.

Practically, however, the number of occasions for baptisms multiplied.

The days for baptism expanded for various reasons. Some people chose other feasts, as if baptism pertained more to festivals in general than to Easter in particular. Others permitted a different day if circumstances made an Easter baptism difficult—illness, travel, the perils of childhood, or a lengthy delay. Others deferred baptism because they could not financially afford it. Consequently, the number of baptismal days multiplied.

People began to think of human life in stages of seven years.

Many writers began to envision a person's life in stages of seven years each. The division assigned a distinct identity to the first seven years of a person's life. In time, though not yet, that distinction would affect the celebration of confirmation and Communion for children.

The Church continued offering infants baptism and Communion; adults also presented themselves for baptism.

The Church continued to defend its practice of infant baptism. Although some candidates for baptism were adults, and although the rites of the Church still assumed that possibility, most of those being baptized were infants. Newly baptized infants continued to receive Communion, but some objections to this practice began to appear.

People believed Communion was inessential for salvation, and the frequency of its reception diminished.

People could receive Communion from childhood, but since they believed baptism alone was necessary for salvation, they regarded Communion as inessential. The frequency of participation in the Eucharist diminished so much that conciliar legislation began to require the reception of Communion at certain intervals.

The bishop's ministry of "consigning" or "confirming" came to include anointing, the imposition of a hand, and prayer for the Holy Spirit.

A homily delivered in late-fifth- or early-sixth-century Gaul solidly influenced the role of confirmation in the life of the Christian. The text explained the difference between baptism and confirmation and demonstrated that the ritual had developed to include three essential features: anointing with chrism, handlaying by the bishop, and prayer for the sevenfold gift of the Holy Spirit. The bishop's action was called alternately "consigning" and "confirming."

The term "confirmation," which originally pertained to the bishop's approval of baptisms by presbyters, came to refer to the strength of the Spirit for the trials of life.

The name of the service, "confirmation," underwent a reinterpretation. Formerly it signified a confirmation by the bishop of the baptism or status of the person's Christianity. But now it was being applied in cases where the bishop had just performed the baptism. "Confirmation" came to mean the strengthening the faithful received from the Holy Spirit for the trials of life. The Latin word *confirmare* supported both interpretations and had also appeared in reference to the activity of the Holy Spirit in influential sources like the New Testament and Ambrose.

When no bishop was present for baptism, confirmation was deferred, but not Communion.

Throughout the development of an independent rite of confirmation, there is no record of the deferral of Communion. Those baptized, at whatever age, remained eligible for Communion and participated in the Eucharist. Those baptized by anyone other than a bishop received confirmation after Communion.

In many places, presbyters had assumed the responsibility of anointing the baptized.

In several areas of the Christian world presbyters again presumed the authority to anoint the baptized. Although this practice never received the approval of Rome, it continued in many places. In many regions, people believed that anointings by presbyters eliminated the need for confirmation by the bishop on an occasion distinct from baptism. This practical but unauthorized solution reduced some difficulties in the ministry of bishops and provided more convenience for the faithful.

In Gaul and Italy, bishops reasserted their responsibility to confirm.

In Gaul, the Council of Paris reaffirmed that bishops, not presbyters, should anoint. In Italy presbyters briefly had permission to anoint in danger of a candidate's death and Pope Gregory approved presbyteral anointings in Sardinia. However, he later enjoined bishops to take up this ministry again.

In Spain, presbyters persisted in spite of Rome's efforts to reserve anointings to bishops.

Presbyters commonly administered anointings in Spain until the Roman-ruled Council of Seville forbade the practice. Still, the custom did not entirely die out.

In Great Britain, presbyters may have anointed, but Rome's influence changed the responsibility for the ministry to bishops.

The evidence in Great Britain is not clear, but it appears from the writings of Bede that presbyters may have anointed there as well. The imposition of the Roman custom eventually prevailed and bishops resumed the responsibility of confirming.

Chapter Five

The Era of Charlemagne

701–828

Under Charlemagne (747–814), king of the Franks and emperor of the West, Christianity flourished along with learning and the arts. In the midst of this cultural renaissance and governmental unification, ritual prayer became more standardized as sacramentaries were compiled and orders of service exchanged hands.

Generally speaking, sacramentaries held prayer texts; orders described how the ritual should be executed. Independent orders of various origins and limited purpose were collected into more useful volumes and somewhat arbitrarily numbered. Together with treatises and councils the rituals presented a sharper picture of the initiation rites of the period.

Rome, Gaul, Milan, the British Isles, and the Germano-Frankish countries all testify to the developing patterns of Christian initiation. These many threads gradually formed a more common tradition in the West. Under Charlemagne baptism held political significance; the baptism of conquered Saxons reflected submission to Frankish rule; failure to accept baptism resulted in death.

During this period two sequences of rites coexisted. The conventional sequence, baptism-anointing-Communion, continued in the West in those circumstances when a bishop presided for the liturgy. However, when a presbyter baptized infants, a more common occurrence, he offered Communion to them at the same time, and they were later presented to the bishop for confirmation. Sources in this period also show the term "confirm" in reference to Communion, the origins of preparing for the reception of Communion, and the persistent variance in the roles of presbyter and bishop in post-baptismal rites.

When bishops presided for baptism, the ritual included anointing and handlaying, then Eucharist.

The centuries-old practice continued. In those instances (increasingly rare) when the bishop presided for baptism at Easter in the cathedral, the other rites of initiation followed in the same ceremony. He administered confirmation and offered the Eucharist to the newly baptized. The practice is clear from many rituals extant from the period.

"Confirming" also came to mean "giving Communion from the cup."

The verb "to confirm" accepted another mutation. During the Carolingian era it came to be used (first in Rome) for the action of giving Communion from the cup. Thus when some of the liturgical orders of the period speak of "confirming," they actually mean giving Communion.

Whether candidates for baptism were infants or adults, they received Communion.

Most of the candidates for baptism were infants. No matter what age the recipient of this sacrament, those baptized were offered Communion in the same ceremony. Some theologians thought that Communion was indeed essential to the Christian life, contrary to the prevailing trend of belief held by those who received Communion infrequently. If the bishop was not present for the baptism (as was most often the case), confirmation was deferred but the newly baptized shared Communion immediately with the rest of the faithful.

Presbyters commonly used rituals for emergency baptism to baptize any infant.

Easter and Pentecost remained the preferred days for baptism, but presbyters commonly baptized shortly after a candidate's birth, using the simplified ritual for emergency baptism, which did not include confirmation but did include Communion.

Since bishops were rarely present at the baptismal Eucharist for infants, their confirmations were deferred.

When those baptized by presbyters were anointed later by a bishop, the conventional sequence of the two rites (anointing then Communion) was reversed. This became the common practice.

Two sequences of rites coexisted; confirmation preceded Eucharist if the bishop was present for baptism; when no bishop was there, confirmation generally followed Eucharist.

In the West, then, two sequences of rites coexisted. Those baptized by a bishop celebrated the rites on one occasion in the manner traditional since about the fourth century. Those baptized by a presbyter received Communion before confirmation.

Other circumstances further diversified the common practices. Some who were baptized by presbyters in the West were never anointed by the bishop and of course experienced no sequence of anointing and Communion at all. In the East, the sequence and occasion of the rites remained unified in the traditional order because presbyters performed all the rites at baptism—including the anointing, which became confirmation in the West—for all candidates, including infants.

People received Communion infrequently after baptism.

As in the previous centuries, the reception of Communion by the faithful remained infrequent. Although they received Communion at baptism most did not continue to participate in the Eucharist regularly throughout their lives.

The Church came to expect a spiritual and moral preparation for Communion, which began to include the confession of sins.

Those who wished to receive Communion on a given occasion were expected to make a spiritual and moral preparation for it. For the first time the Church explicitly began to connect the confession of sins to the reception of Communion at intervals in one's life.

The Church expected bishops to travel throughout their dioceses each year to confirm those baptized by presbyters.

The number of those unconfirmed was beginning to cause some anxiety in the Church. Bishops were not completely available to all those eligible for this ceremony. Some did not circulate throughout their dioceses to confirm. Consequently, councils began to require bishops to visit the various population centers of their dioceses at regular intervals.

In some traditions from northern Italy, Gaul, and the British Isles, the baptism by presbyters sufficed without a later confirmation by a bishop.

In spite of Roman efforts to stop the practice of post-baptismal anointings by presbyters in place of deferred confirmation by bishops, the practice continued. Evidence for presbyteral anointings without confirmation by bishops surfaced in the Carolingian era in northern Italy, Gaul, and Ireland.

Chapter Six

Regulating Initiation

829–964

During the ninth and tenth centuries the Church made further efforts to regulate the practices surrounding the reception of baptism, confirmation, and Eucharist. Between the time of the sixth Council of Paris (829) and the probable completion of the *Roman-Germanic Pontifical* (964), the increase of canonical legislation and the unification of ritual texts indicate that the variety of customs disquieted Church leadership.

Western Europe was suffering from too much variety. Charlemagne's empire disintegrated, and with it the cultural and ecclesiastical unity it had imposed. The increasingly regular incursions of the Vikings, a growing East-West schism, and the expansion of Islam threatened the Church's unity and clarified the need to disseminate orders and sacramentaries. Such instability even would have complicated the bishops' ability and desire to make regular visitations for confirmation. The search for conformity in initiation practices appears as one attempt to restore some order in a society threatened by change.

The now-familiar initiation sequences continued: infants and adults received baptism, confirmation, and Eucharist at the Easter Vigil whenever the bishop presided. In the more common instances when presbyters baptized, confirmation was deferred. The celebration of confirmation apart from baptism received its own ritual for the first time. Infants continued to receive Communion, but the practice of including Eucharist with baptism began to wane; the sequence of confirmation and Communion then became harder to predict. Since the ministry of confirmation was restricted to bishops, the frequency of its celebration lessened.

The ninth- and tenth-century pontificals called for bishops to preside over baptism, confirmation, and Eucharist at Easter and Pentecost in the cathedral.

During this period several pontificals with rubrics and prayers were compiled for the use of bishops. Whenever they described the rite of baptism, the ceremony included the administration of confirmation and the giving of Communion in liturgies reserved for Easter and Pentecost at the cathedral. Although the instances must have been rare, the consistent appearance of this rite in the pontificals suggests that they must have been used to some degree.

Permissions for presbyters to baptize in other places on other occasions proliferated.

Although the preference for Easter and Pentecost baptisms remained in force the permissions for presbyters to baptize on other occasions proliferated. Sickness, danger of death, and other necessities reinforced the trend to baptize infants soon after birth, not in connection with the preferred feast days.

When presbyters baptized, which was quite common, confirmation was deferred, but they were instructed to offer Communion.

The same pontificals that preserved the conventional sequence of baptism-confirmation-Eucharist and the single occasion for their celebration also included a rubric concerning Communion for those occasions when a presbyter led the entire ceremony. Its appearance indicates that the books were enjoying usage beyond cathedrals and that the custom of presbyters baptizing had become so common that a rubric was needed to clarify the procedure. This rubric for presbyters explicitly stated that, in the absence of a bishop at baptism, confirmation was deferred, but the presbyter should offer Communion to the newly baptized.

Infants continued to be baptized and receive Communion.

The custom of baptizing infants continued, driven by the fear of condemnation for the many infants who died before entering their childhood years. As already noted, many orders of baptism specifically called for the Communion of infants.

Some traditions deferred infant Communion from baptism.

A growing concern and debate materialized over those who died after baptism and without Communion. The number of texts suggests that the practice of offering baptism without Communion—whether out of convenience or preference—was beginning to grow. Even though the liturgical books requested Communion for the baptized, it appears that it did not always happen, and Eucharist began to be separated from baptism.

The sequence of confirmation and Communion for those baptized by anyone but a bishop became less clear.

Practices began to diverge even further. Bishops were expected to offer baptism, confirmation, and Communion at one ceremony. Presbyters were expected to defer confirmation. Some presbyters were apparently also deferring Communion. Once confirmation and Communion both detached from baptism it became difficult for later generations to determine which of the two preceded the other during this period. The occasion for confirmation was tied to the arrival of the bishop, which theoretically could have happened before or after the first reception of Communion.

Bishops frequently confirmed after baptism, either a week later or on the occasion of a pastoral visit.

As Communion began to be detached from baptism when the presbyter served as minister, so confirmation began to be detached from baptism when the bishop served as minister. Several incidents indicate that in some places, probably inspired by the widespread practice of deferred confirmation for those baptized by presbyters, confirmation also began to be deferred for those baptized by bishops.

Chorbishops and presbyters attempted to share the ministry of confirmation, but the Church restricted it to bishops.

Disagreements over the proper minister of confirmation resurfaced with the return of chorbishops to the Church's ministry. Appointed to assist bishops, their appearance created many conflicts over their authority. Many of them exercised the ministry of confirmation, but the Church again attempted to reserve this to bishops alone. Even the post-baptismal anointing by presbyters had to be restrained again. Although the Church's hierarchy restricted confirmation to the ministry of bishops, many efforts were made to share it with other ministers.

Many of the faithful were never confirmed.

Without chorbishops to assist, with fewer baptisms happening at cathedrals, with bishops neglecting their duty to visit the diocese every year, many people were never confirmed. Church leaders exhorted the faithful to be confirmed. Some effort was made to ensure that confirmations would take place while the child was still in infancy. Even so, it appears that many of the faithful were never confirmed at all.

Chapter Seven

Pastoral Concerns

965–1214

Between the mid-tenth and the early thirteenth centuries pastoral concerns began to affect the pattern of celebration for baptism, confirmation, and Communion. In the years between the *Roman-Germanic Pontifical* (965) and the Council of Lateran IV (1215), civilization enjoyed a period of relative prosperity and cultural revival. The increased contacts among countries and the growing central authority of the papacy (notably under the reforms of Gregory VII) produced an atmosphere in which the sacramental rites could universally adjust to some practical concerns.

Some pastoral decisions had already come into place. Fear of infant mortality led to baptism shortly after birth. The unavailability of bishops at every baptism led to delayed confirmation.

Newer developments became more customary. The infrequent reception of Communion led to a decreased offering of the baptismal Eucharist. The inconvenience of getting confirmed caused many of the faithful to disregard the sacrament. The delay in celebrating confirmation and Communion led to a desire for some modest catechetical preparation. The need for ritual texts led to printed rites of baptism for presbyters and of confirmation for bishops.

Vestiges of the conventional sequence of initiation rites endured along with other notions. Although evidence for infant Communion persisted, giving Eucharist to infants at baptism continued to wane. Some initiation rites conducted by presbyters were still considered complete, and many faithful were not confirmed by a bishop. So although the conventional sequence of initiation rites survived in some instances, confirmation and the first reception of Communion were displaced with more frequency, their sequence became more erratic, and children received one, the other, both, or neither after baptism.

When a bishop was present for baptism, he confirmed the newly baptized, who also received Communion at the liturgy.

The missals and pontificals of this period continued the practice of publishing baptismal rituals that called for confirmation and Communion when the bishop was present. In those instances, at least on paper, all three rites took place at the same ceremony as they had in the past.

When no bishop was present for baptism, the presbyter offered the newly baptized Communion, and confirmation was deferred.

Confirmation was still firmly attached to the ministry of bishops. Therefore, if a bishop was not present for the baptism, confirmation was deferred, but the one baptized received Communion. The rubrics for baptismal Communion in the absence of the bishop appeared in all the major rituals of this period, indicating how common the situation had become.

Theologians and Church councils agreed that children should be baptized as soon as possible.

Although Easter and Pentecost were still upheld as traditional days for baptism, in practice everyone agreed that children should be baptized as soon as possible after birth. The fear of their death and the desire to share the benefits of baptism prompted many statements favoring the baptism of infants soon after birth.

After baptism, infants and children received Communion infrequently.

Evidence abounds that infants and children received Communion not only at their baptism but at other occasions in their young Christian life. However, it appears that the occasions for Communion remained infrequent, causing some concern from theologians and Church leaders.

The Church offered Communion to newly baptized infants less frequently.

In spite of a long tradition of giving Communion to the newly baptized, the practice began to wane. Many people believed the reception of Communion was not necessary—an opinion that brought comfort to parents of children who died young. The belief also fit the pattern of infrequent reception of Communion. Resistance to receiving Communion deepened as reverence for the Eucharist emphasized the unworthiness of the worshiper. The number of the baptized who never received Communion before death apparently increased.

Preparation for the infrequent reception of Communion included catechesis and repentance.

The Church increased its efforts to have those intending to receive Communion make a proper preparation for it. At this time some form of catechesis began to precede Communion, at least the recitation of the Lord's Prayer and the Creed. People were also expected to demonstrate their willingness to repent from their sins before sharing in the eucharistic table.

Orders of service for confirmation apart from baptism appeared for the first time.

The actual ceremony of confirmation apart from baptism must have existed for centuries. However, since no independent ritual text prior to this period has been preserved, none probably existed. The development of a rite of confirmation at this point of its history indicates that the ceremony had taken on an important and permanent part of the Church's ministry.

The Church perceived confirmation more as a responsibility of bishops than a part of baptismal initiation.

For centuries the age of confirmation fluctuated, depending entirely on the availability of the bishop. The common age of confirmation began to drift away from infancy to allow for catechetical preparation and for children to remember the event. Its interpretation had nothing to do with baptismal initiation.

As theologians interpreted confirmation as strengthening, they justified its celebration at an age later than baptism, even at adolescence.

More and more theologians interpreted confirmation as a strengthening for the moral fight of the Christian life. During this period the first suggestion was made that confirmation should be received in adolescence, an opinion that would gain wider acceptance many centuries later.

The Church expressed no preference for the sequence of confirmation and the first reception of Communion.

Throughout this period, when the sequence of confirmation and the first reception of Communion began to vary more considerably, the Church expressed no preference for one sequence over the other. Most of the faithful experienced confirmation not as an initiation rite, but as a ceremony during the visit of the bishop. Its relationship to the first reception of Communion never appeared in the discussion.

Some places did not require confirmation by a bishop after baptism by presbyters.

Once again in this period, the opinion endured that no confirmation by a bishop was necessary after the baptismal rites performed by a presbyter. Even though this interpretation never won approval from Rome, in many parts of the Christian world the custom continued and even seemed supported by liturgical texts.

Many people were never confirmed, probably due to inconvenience.

Pastors were encouraged to have their people receive confirmation, to do so only once, and to be prepared for it. Such directives imply that many people were choosing not to be confirmed at all, probably due to the irregular visits of the bishop and the inconvenience of participating in the ceremony whenever and wherever it was held. Consequently, concerning the sequence of rites at this period, some who were baptized were not confirmed at all and some probably did not receive Communion.

Chapter Eight

The Age of Discretion

1215–1519

In the centuries before the beginning of the Reformation (1519) two significant changes happened in an otherwise consistent pattern of initiation practice. The baptismal Eucharist disappeared and the Church expected a child to manifest "discretion" before receiving Communion for the first time.

At the very moment the Church enjoyed extensive power, authority, and uniformity, the troubles of society (e.g., the Black Death and the Hundred Years War) foreshadowed an era of scandal and corruption (e.g., the Avignon Papacy and the divisions resulting from the Reformation). Meanwhile, as devotion to the Eucharist deepened, scrupulosity increased over who could receive it. In an era when universities were being founded, when the education of children was becoming more accessible, and when Thomism created a growing intellectual confidence, the Church reserved the Eucharist to those who could manifest some understanding of it and who could demonstrate appropriate moral behavior.

A canon of the Fourth Lateran Council (1215) regarding annual confession became the catalyst for these developments: the disappearance of infant Communion at baptism, the expectation of catechetical preparation for the reception of the Eucharist, and the age and practice of confirmation and its sequence with First Communion. The Church entered its own "age of discretion."

During this period references to full initiation of infants at Easter and Pentecost dwindled as the baptismal Eucharist disappeared. Lateran IV's call for discretion and an annual confession provoked widespread reaction, as the community delayed a child's First Communion until age ten to twelve. The age for confirmation continued to vary, and for the first time people began to promote its reception prior to First Communion.

Infants received confirmation at their baptism on rare occasions when the bishop was present, and Communion was generally deferred.

The church in the West finally stopped giving Communion to infants at baptism during this period. Prior to this time anyone, regardless of age, would be eligible for the baptismal Eucharist. Although some theologians of the period knew of infant Communion, the practice virtually ceased. In the rare instances when a bishop presided over a baptism, he confirmed at the same time, but even then Communion for the infants he baptized was deferred. (Older children could receive Communion at baptism.)

Although Church legislation still favored baptism on Easter and Pentecost, people had children baptized shortly after birth, causing confirmation to be delayed.

The designation of Easter and Pentecost baptisms not only favored the ancient festivals, but also the ancient role of the bishop. Baptism was especially fitting to be celebrated on those days for the bishop's convenience and participation. The bishop could still confirm those whom he baptized, even infants, but most people had their children baptized by a presbyter shortly after the birth of the child, causing little participation in the traditional baptismal days and the deferral of confirmation.

Substitutes were devised in place of the baptismal Eucharist for infants.

In the past infants commonly received Communion under the form of wine. During this period, in a few places, another ceremony was sometimes included as a substitute for the Eucharist; for example, parents looked at a consecrated host or children received unconsecrated wine.

The Fourth Lateran Council required those at the "years of discretion" to confess their sins annually and to receive Communion reverently at least during Easter.

The Fourth Lateran Council (1215) served as a watershed for the history of the age of the candidate and the sequence of the sacraments of baptism, confirmation, and Eucharist. It decreed that every Christian should confess his or her sins once a year after reaching the "years of discretion." It also asked people to fulfill their penance and receive Communion during the season of Easter. The council did not require the deferral of Communion to the age of discretion or confession before every Communion, but it set up a rhythm that allowed those applications. Also, by requesting that the Christian receive communion "reverently," Lateran IV laid the groundwork for making devotion a part of a child's preparation for the first reception of Communion.

Many equated "years of discretion" with "a capacity for deceit"—phrases that applied to the confession of sins, but remained imprecise.

The Fourth Lateran Council used the phrase "years of discretion" to describe the approximate age at which annual Communion was required. Many theologians equated it with the phrase "a capacity for deceit." Those expressions pertained to the ability to commit sin responsibly, and hence the need for confession. The Church did not define the age more precisely, probably because of the variations in human development. Theological opinion generally placed the age between seven and fourteen.

Although Lateran IV did not call for it, people began deferring First Communion to "years of discretion" and preceding it with confession.

The Fourth Lateran Council did not forbid giving Communion to infants before the years of discretion, but the practice virtually ceased after the council. Since an annual Communion was not required before the years of discretion, people stopped offering it before then. Furthermore, since the faithful were confessing their sins before receiving Communion (a practice made more possible by the infrequency of reception), the Church began to expect confession even before First Communion.

The Communion of infants, once expected, became forbidden.

The custom of infant Communion completely changed. Formerly infants were expected to receive Communion at their baptism. Then the practice waned. Finally it was forbidden. Thomas Aquinas argued that Communion was not necessary for salvation, relieving any sense of urgency to offer it to the very young. He also expressed concern about the danger of young children spilling the precious blood of Christ. Pope Leo X refused to permit the practice of infant Communion to resolve a dispute in Bohemia.

In some places a substitute for Communion was offered to children.

In place of giving Communion to young children between their baptism and their years of discretion, many places began to substitute "blessed bread" or a drink of unconsecrated wine. Others opposed the practice.

The Church expected people to be catechized prior to receiving Communion.

Increasingly the Church expected people to receive catechesis before receiving Communion. Since they were not required to receive Communion until reaching years of discretion, many did not begin receiving Communion until then. That created an opportunity for catechesis to precede the first reception of Communion.

Fees attached to Communion may have deferred the age of its first reception.

Church leaders abhorred the practice, but some places still attached a fee to those who received Communion. The custom probably contributed to the further deferral in the age of sharing in the Eucharist, since some people could not afford to have several children participate.

Children received Communion for the first time around ages ten to twelve, though exceptions were many.

No ceremony had yet developed for the first reception of Communion, but when the question of age arose, theologians most often recommended a range from ten or twelve. Alexander of Hales first required the "use of reason" for children to share the Eucharist. As "years of discretion" pertained more to the capacity for sin, "use of reason" promoted the ability to discern the body and blood of Christ from ordinary food and drink. The two terms reflected the Church's twin concerns for behavioral and intellectual preparation for Communion. Some shared the Eucharist for the first time as young as age seven, others at eighteen or older.

Bishops continued visiting their dioceses to confirm those baptized by others.

Bishops continued their practice of touring the diocese to confirm those who had already been baptized by another minister. As they did so the ritual for confirmation evolved even further.

*The age of candidates for confirmation varied from infancy to adulthood,
but seven was suggested for the first time.*

Never in the past had confirmation been attached to an age. It re-
lated only to an occasion: the availability of the bishop. When he
baptized or visited those already baptized he would confirm. Consequently, the age of candidates for confirmation up to this point varied from infancy to adulthood. But during this period, the age of
confirmation began to become an issue. The Synod of Cologne
(1280) first urged confirmation for those age seven and older. Although opinions about the proper age for confirmation varied considerably at this time, eventually seven came to be regarded as the
minimum age.

*Theologians strengthened their interpretation of confirmation as a
sacrament that prepared one for the struggles of life.*

With the establishment of a minimum age for confirmation came a
stronger interpretation that this sacrament prepared the faithful for the
struggles of life. It had lost its close relationship to baptism. Although
confirmation still pertained to the ministry of bishops it more widely received an additional interpretation as a sacrament to be celebrated after
infancy, one that prepared the recipient to live faithfully the Christian
life.

*The giving of a slap and the taking of a name were added to the
confirmation ritual.*

In the development of the confirmation ritual William Durandus recommended that the bishop lightly slap the cheek of the one to be confirmed. This gesture, drawn from the ritual for the blessing of a knight,
indicated one's willingness to confess Christ. Bishops could impose a
new name at confirmation. The permission answered a concern that
some baptismal names did not adequately represent Christian sanctity
and virtue.

Many were not being confirmed at all.

The proliferation of texts admonishing presbyters to urge the faithful to bring their children to be confirmed indicates that many were not
being confirmed at all. Confirmation demanded cooperation among
bishops, presbyters, and parents. But many of the baptized apparently
were never confirmed.

Some expressed the preference that confirmation precede the first reception of Eucharist, probably to encourage people to be confirmed.

Prior to this period, the Church showed little interest in the sequence of confirmation and the first reception of Communion, since it perceived no relationship between the two sacraments. It was more important that the bishop serve as minister of confirmation than that a particular sequence be observed. However, in isolated instances during this period local churches recommended that confirmation precede sharing in the Eucharist, probably because it would encourage the reception of confirmation.

Chapter Nine

Reformation

1520–1592

The Reformation polarized religious camps, bringing theological reform to the followers of Martin Luther and a reactionary call to uniformity for the followers of the pope. Luther's treatise on sacraments limited their number to two, baptism and Eucharist, but the Council of Trent restated the Roman tradition that there were seven.

In the brief period between the unfolding of the Reformation (1520) and the appearance of First Communion rituals in the Roman Catholic Church (1593), the Roman Church maintained its pattern of celebrating infant baptism with deferred confirmation and Eucharist. The Reformation increased interest in catechetical formation and in pastoral care for children, which prepared the way for the innovation of First Communion rituals. The Church's interest in education was nursed by the polemics of the Reformation and a growing interest in the sciences.

Throughout this period infant baptism was celebrated mostly in isolation of confirmation and Eucharist. Confession entered the sequence of sacraments for children. Children prepared for the first reception of Communion. Confirmation was being deferred to age seven. The sequence of confirmation and First Communion held little importance.

Both confirmation and first Communion were customarily deferred from infant baptism.

The custom developing in the previous few centuries persisted. Those baptized received the sacrament apart from confirmation and

Eucharist. Although the Roman Missal permitted baptisms on Holy Saturday according to the traditional format, the instances of full initiation that day must have been rare.

The Church began to expect confession to precede Communion, including First Communion.

Under the influence of the Fourth Lateran Council and pastors like Charles Borromeo, the Church raised its expectations of confession before Communion, even before First Communion.

Preparation for First Communion included confession and evidence of moral and intellectual development.

Theologians agreed that Communion should be reserved for those who had shown intellectual capacity to discern the difference in foods and moral capacity to discern right from wrong. Moral behavior, intellectual development, confession of sins, and devotion to the Eucharist had become requirements for sharing Communion.

Confirmation appeared more as a blessing of bishops and an occasion for catechesis rather than a rite of initiation.

As the ritual of confirmation developed it settled into ritual books among the blessings given by bishops. Practically it served as an opportunity to provide catechesis. It bore no connection to baptism and was not called initiation.

Confirmation became associated with age seven; Communion with age ten or after.

Church councils more generally recommended that confirmation not be received prior to age seven, although some exceptions existed. The Church still lacked any universal legislation on this topic. The age for First Communion varied, but children generally did not share the Eucharist until age ten or later.

The sequence of confirmation and the first reception of Communion remained in flux.

Those who received all these sacraments probably received them in this order: baptism, confirmation, Eucharist. But there were many exceptions since some received Communion before confirmation and others did not ever receive either confirmation or Communion or both.

Reformation churches developed confirmation to conclude a period of catechesis and First Communion as a public ceremony for children.

The churches of the Reform did not regard confirmation as a sacrament, but they retained it as a useful ritual. Although these churches did not work in concert on this particular point, they generally developed confirmation as the conclusion to a period of catechesis. They also established a public ceremony of First Communion for children. These ideas originated outside the Catholic Church.

Chapter Ten

The Ritualization of First Communion

1593–1773

Group First Communion in the Roman Catholic Church first appeared in France in 1593. By the time legislation on confirmation intensified (1774), the ceremony was firmly rooted in the Church. In fact, within fifty years of its appearance, First Communion had become quite elaborate and intensely popular. It arose in a time and place when the faithful adopted other devotions, like prayers to the Sacred Heart and processions of the Blessed Sacrament. This piety spread when the scientific revolution and the enlightenment were threatening traditional religious belief. The expansion of secular education advanced the concern for religious education.

The ritualizing of First Communion evolved from the simplification of baptismal rites for infants and the expansion of rites for children. Infant baptism remained the norm; some Communion-like customs accompanied it in a few places, but both confirmation and Eucharist were deferred. Confession of sins became part of every Catholic's life beginning from youth. The age of confirmation had settled at seven or older, and Communion around age ten or older.

First Communion rituals, formerly unheard of in Church history, became immensely appealing to the faithful. Since the Church desired better catechesis for everyone, especially for children, instruction became part of the preparation for Communion and influenced the popular establishment of the age of First Communion around ten to fourteen. However, with the influence of Jansenism, some delayed the age for First Communion even further. Throughout this period, parishes developed an elaborate ritual for First Communion, drawing on eucharistic piety, the desire to pass on the faith to a new generation of children, and the devotional inspiration that could be drawn from the simple faith of children.

Some discussion of the sequence of confirmation and Communion also appeared in this period, as well as a growing disparity between Eastern rite baptism and the Western practices.

In the West, children were generally baptized shortly after birth, without confirmation or Communion.

The custom of the previous centuries continued. Most born into Catholic homes in the West were baptized shortly after birth. Their confirmation and first reception of Communion came later. Only rarely would two or three of these sacraments be celebrated at once.

Some baptisms included a substitute for the Eucharist.

The long tradition of offering Communion at the baptism of infants was remembered well enough in some places by continuing the custom of offering some substitute for the Eucharist at the baptism of infants— whether bringing children to the altar or offering them unconsecrated wine.

The Church expected the frequent confession of sins once one obtained the use of reason.

The faithful were expected to make frequent use of the sacrament of confession each year, partly to prepare for sharing the Eucharist.

The Church began to require confession before First Communion.

Even children too young to receive Communion were expected to confess their sins. Hence confession was expected before First Communion, and children could have had several years' experience of confession before sharing the Eucharist.

Confirmation was forbidden before the age of seven, except in extraordinary circumstances.

According to local Church councils of this period, seven generally remained the minimum age for confirmation. The confirmation of infants was always permitted in extraordinary circumstances.

Some preferred an age closer to twelve for confirmation.

Some councils preferred an age for confirmation closer to twelve. During this period no other proposed age for the sacrament entered the discussion.

The age of the first reception of Communion fluctuated. Some allowed it at the use of reason; others preferred age ten to fourteen after some catechesis; still others waited longer, including those influenced by Jansenism.

The age for the first reception of Communion continued to fluctuate because of the various interpretations of the age for the use of reason. Although ages ten to fourteen remained a common recommendation, some preferred younger ages and some older. The influence of Jansenism caused many to consider children unworthy for Communion until a much later age.

The catechesis of children became preparation for a First Communion liturgy; it included confession of sins and fostering a devotional eucharistic piety.

Children were expected to complete a catechesis as part of their preparation for First Communion. This included instruction on the meaning of the Eucharist, but also a moral reflection leading to confession of sins and the fostering of a piety conducive to adoration of the Eucharist, rather than to its frequent reception.

First Communion rituals began in parishes and spread as a grassroots movement through dioceses and religious orders.

The idea for Catholic First Communion rituals began in parishes. The elaborate ceremonies caught on within fifty years of the earliest records. Gradually dioceses and religious communities began to regulate First Communions, but Rome never authorized a rite of First Communion. The entire custom spread from personal experiences.

The sequence of sacraments generally proceeded from baptism at infancy to confirmation after age seven, to Communion sometime later, though there were exceptions.

The occasion for confirmation was still connected with the availability of the bishop, but it was not recommended for children younger than seven. The recommended minimum age for Communion was a little higher. In theory, then, those baptized in infancy probably received confirmation next and finally Communion at a later occasion. But there were exceptions.

Some preference for the sequence of confirmation and First Communion started to become explicit, without consensus.

Discussion began to emerge about the sequence of confirmation and First Communion. Some preferred it one way; others in reverse. The preferences garnered little attention during this period.

The Eastern rites generally continued offering the three sacraments together for infants.

Although the rites of baptism, confirmation, and Communion had mutated in the West, the custom in the East had generally remained the same: all three sacraments were administered at once, even for infants.

The Western church made attempts to bring the East to conformity.

Because the practice in the East diverged so much from that in the West, the Roman Church made some unsuccessful attempts to bring the traditions together. The awareness of this diversity created some discomfort in the West.

Chapter Eleven

Sequence

1774–1909

By the late eighteenth century, opinions surfaced more frequently regarding the sequence of confirmation and First Communion. The question had not fully matured prior to this time since the First Communion ritual had only recently developed; in addition, the catechesis in preparation for sacraments expanded.

The dominant historical context for this period includes the influence of revolutionary thought, the development and spread of secular and scientific ideologies, and the influence of nationalism. The Church suffered a decline in temporal influence and a rise in anti-clerical attack. Romanticism affirmed the emotional appeal of faith. The Church, under popes like Gregory XVI and Pius IX, responded with an affirmation of authority and triumphalism. The rise of significant national educational systems cultivated an ever stronger emphasis on catechetical preparation.

Several features characterized the sacramental practice of the West between the development of legislation regarding confirmation (1774) and the lowering of the age for First Communion (1910). Confirmation was generally not administered to those under age seven, except in extraordinary conditions. The West did not grant exceptions for First Communion, however, for which the preferred age remained around ten to fourteen. Regional controversies over the age of First Communion set the stage for the promulgation of a universal policy. Rome refused to declare that adolescence was the minimum age for First Communion. The influence of Jansenism, the neglect of pastors and families, and the frequency of Communion urged on the faithful delayed the preparation of some children.

In addition, Eastern rites offered confirmation and Communion regularly to infants. Opinions differed about the sequence of confirmation and Communion; although many local councils preferred Communion to precede confirmation, Rome favored the reverse.

In the West the baptism of infants was celebrated apart from confirmation and Eucharist.

No change in baptismal practice emerged during this period. In general, the faithful brought their infants to be baptized. Confirmation and the first reception of Communion would follow later.

Rome restricted infant confirmations to extraordinary circumstances, but the practice endured in several regions.

Infants could be confirmed in exceptional circumstances, but in some regions the custom had more generally taken root. Spain, Switzerland, the Sandwich Isles, and Latin America all had common instances of infant confirmation, a practice that Rome tried to minimize.

Confirmation was generally administered to children age seven or older, after they had received some instruction to prepare them for the struggles of the Christian life.

The usual practice of confirmation continued. Children baptized in infancy who had reached at least age seven were candidates for confirmation. They received catechetical formation for a sacrament that was to prepare them to live out the Christian life.

The age of confirmation implied its association with penance, not with baptism.

Confirmation had long lost its association with baptism. Its recommended age implied it shared something in common with sacraments like penance, administered when the recipient was capable of catechesis.

The age of First Communion remained around ten to fourteen, but some leaders preferred a later age, and some people never received the Eucharist.

Again, the "years of discretion" or the age of "the use of reason" was never narrowly defined by the universal Church. However, a growing opinion named ages ten to fourteen as the years most appropriate for the first reception of Communion. Some preferred even later ages, but this met resistance. Some never did receive Communion after being baptized.

Both confirmation and First Communion became opportunities for some children to profess for themselves the faith professed by others at their infant baptism.

Since confirmation and First Communion had become celebrations in childhood for those baptized in infancy, these sacramental events became opportunities for catechesis. Some of the faithful interpreted these events as occasions for children to express for themselves the faith others had professed for them when they were baptized as infants.

Rome settled controversies in Rouen, Annecy, and Strasbourg by permitting Communion at a young age.

Pastoral dilemmas surfaced in three different dioceses during this period: Rouen, Annecy, and Strasbourg. In each case an effort was made to forbid First Communion to children below the age of twelve or thirteen. The cases, which caused controversy within dioceses between the bishop and his priests, went to Rome on appeal. In each case, Rome refused to forbid Communion to children below age twelve, in keeping with directives from the Fourth Lateran Council and the aversion to defining the age of discretion.

The preparation for First Communion received support from Church leadership and influenced the development of catechetical materials.

Catechetical materials were developed to help Church leadership prepare children for the first reception of Communion. The event became an opportunity for the education of children, producing broad support.

First Communion ceremonies gained widespread popularity for the piety they instilled in the faithful and the memories they created for the children.

The elaborate ceremonies that accompanied First Communions created an indelible memory for parents and children alike. The services were designed in a way to capitalize on eucharistic piety and to create favorable sentiment for the event. A successful First Communion ceremony created an emotional response from the participants.

Eastern rites continued offering chrismation and Communion at baptism, a practice the West continued to resist.

The disparity of confirmation practices between the East and West became even more evident. Some in the West looked with longing on the unchanged practice in the East, where chrismation accompanied baptism, but Rome insisted that the confirmation of infants in the East was a privilege it tolerated, not one it advocated.

In the West, some preferred that confirmation should follow First Communion to enhance the effect of its preparation and celebration.

Within a short space of time a number of councils from different parts of the Catholic West promoted Communion before confirmation. Their reasons included the reception of more abundant fruit from confirmation, local tradition, the greater intelligence and piety of the children, the memory of the event, instruction and preparation for fighting for the faith, and for the completion of religious instruction.

Others preferred confirmation should precede First Communion because of the tradition of the Church.

An alternate opinion preferred confirmation before First Communion. Rome strongly led the way for this preference, reshaping the decisions of some local councils that had originally framed the reverse. Pope Leo XIII himself spoke favorably of confirmation before First Communion. Proponents never mentioned the relationship of confirmation to baptism. They displayed some reverence for the ancient custom of the Church and some resistance to new developments.

Chapter Twelve

The Diversification of Tradition

1910–2000

In the final century of the second millennium the participant age of confirmation diversified considerably and its temporal sequence with First Communion remained unstable in the West. Indicative of the Church's inability to unify the theology of confirmation and reluctance to reabsorb the ancient tradition of infant Communion, parish celebrations bore testimony to inconsistencies in the Church's theory and practice.

During this century two world wars stretched people's capacity for stability and peace. The globalization of corporations evidenced the profitability of unity. The Second Vatican Council brought the Church into a broader dialogue with the secular world. The hunger for unity within the Church revealed differences needing to be overcome, even in the way the initiation rites were understood and celebrated.

The sacraments underwent considerable scrutiny. Confirmation and Eucharist were restored to the baptismal rites, but only for adults. *Quam singulari,* the watershed publication that began this period (1910), lowered the age of First Communion for children. The age for confirmation remained at seven or above, but permissions for younger confirmations endured in certain circumstances, even as the clamor for older confirmation intensified. The sequence of confirmation and First Communion came under more scrutiny. The Church recovered a sense of "sacraments of initiation." The insistent requirement to confess sins before First Communion placed reconciliation in the midst of the initiation sacraments.

45

By the end of the millennium, the Church's initiation rites showed influences from the earliest centuries, the Middle Ages, and from modern society, making the twentieth century a microcosm of the previous nineteen in its variety of practice and controversy.

Confirmation and Eucharist were restored to the baptismal rite of adults.

The restoration of the catechumenate to the Church in the late twentieth century brought baptism, confirmation, and the first reception of Communion together again. Even though the possibility of having the three rites in the same Easter celebration existed in previous centuries, it now gained greater acceptance because a presbyter possessed the faculty to confirm in circumstances of adult initiation.

Infant baptism included only a vestige of the Communion rite.

After the Second Vatican Council the rite of infant baptism was revised. It included neither confirmation nor Communion, but the anointing with chrism and the recitation of the Lord's Prayer came with texts alluding to those sacraments. The liturgy remembers the former custom of offering all three sacraments to infants.

In 1910 Quam singulari *set the age of First Communion around seven by uniting the age of discretion with that of the use of reason.*

In the previous decades, Rome had revealed a tendency not to raise too high the age of First Communion. In 1910 the Sacred Congregation of the Discipline of the Sacraments issued its watershed decree, *Quam singulari,* with the approval of Pope Pius X, a decree that united the terms "age of discretion" and "use of reason" and established them both around age seven. This created serious implications for the sequence of the sacraments and the nature of preparation for First Communion.

At first the new age of First Communion was criticized for lowering catechetical standards.

The initial reaction to the decree did not support it. Pastors and those in catechetical ministry resisted what appeared to be an administrative decision from Rome. Younger children could not learn what older children had. Catechetical standards for First Communion were being lowered.

Church leaders modified the preparation required for First Communion.

New catechetical guidelines appeared to obtain uniformity in the wake of this dramatic pastoral change. Catechists abandoned the desire to teach younger children the same amount of material that older children had been learning. Instead, they adjusted the preparation to the capacity of the child.

At first some younger children celebrated First Communion in private and a public solemn Communion when they were older.

In some places, young children made their First Communion in smaller, more private ceremonies. Then, when they reached the traditional age of the past few centuries, a solemn celebration of communion was held for their class. This permitted the continuation of the former practice, except that the children were not actually celebrating a First Communion at the public gathering.

Gradually the First Communion ceremony for adolescents was celebrated by younger children, virtually unchanged.

The First Communion ritual formerly designed for adolescents was assigned to younger children, virtually without change. Pastors and catechists made no adaptations in the dress, demeanor, or ritual for the age or capacity of younger children, because the overall effect of First Communion ceremonies could still be achieved.

Although the recommended age for confirmation remained around seven, many interpreted it as a sacrament of commitment and deferred it to adolescence.

The Church never established a universal age of confirmation because it required the presence of a bishop, whose visitation schedule remained unpredictable. The recommended age for confirmation continued to fluctuate in the West. Some dioceses interpreted it as a sacrament of commitment and deferred its celebration until children had reached adolescence. However, as recently as 1952 Rome did not permit the deferral of all confirmations beyond age seven.

In the West, presbyters received the faculty to confirm in many circumstances.

The practice in the West began to partially imitate that in the East, whereby presbyters obtained the faculty to confirm. Western presbyters received permission to confirm in danger of death, in mission areas, and ultimately at adult baptisms. They still did not receive permission to confirm in every instance of infant baptism.

Vatican II began calling baptism, confirmation, and Eucharist "sacraments of initiation," but the sequence of confirmation and First Communion for those baptized as infants continued to alternate.

The Second Vatican Council eventually adopted the expression "sacraments of initiation" to refer to baptism, confirmation, and the first reception of Communion, in any order and on any number of occasions. Since the occasions for these sacraments had not been united, the sequence of confirmation and First Communion for those baptized as infants continued to alternate.

Rome expected confession to precede First Communion, over the objections of many in pastoral work.

The only sequence of sacraments that Rome required of children was confession before Communion—for those baptized as infants. However, since the Church only required the confession of serious sins, many wondered how this applied to candidates for First Communion. Pastoral efforts to defer the sacrament of reconciliation after First Communion met resistance from Rome.

The Eastern rites continued offering chrismation and Communion at baptism.

Meanwhile, in the Eastern rites celebration of the three sacraments remained together. In general, infants in the East continued to receive confirmation and Communion at their baptism.

Conclusions

The age of candidates for baptism, confirmation, and the first reception of Communion has shifted throughout history. The sequence of confirmation and First Communion has long remained unstable in the West. The changes have kept several issues in sacramental practice unresolved.

A key difficulty in setting a direction for the celebration of these sacraments arises from the attempt to establish the meaning of the term "initiation." Throughout the history of these sacraments the term has been used, abused, trumpeted, and ignored. It defies precise definition. In the early Church the term generally applied to the baptismal rites, not to those that were displaced from baptism. In the Middle Ages the term virtually disappeared. When Vatican II recovered the term "initiation," it pertained to baptism, confirmation, and the first reception of the Eucharist, even though these sacraments were not necessarily celebrated on the same occasion. This effectively gave the late-twentieth-century Church two perceptions of initiation, one on a single occasion and the other protracted over many years. The two perceptions do not blend well. Although confirmation and First Communion are commonly called sacraments of initiation, the Church has not adequately explained what that means when they are celebrated separately from baptism.

These conclusions will summarize the fluctuations in age for the reception of these sacraments and the many sequences tolerated in their history. They will also identify important issues the Church still faces and propose solutions.

Summary

In the history of the Western church, how old were people when they were baptized and confirmed and received First Communion?

Baptism has always been offered to infants and adults. Although the evidence for infant baptism in the first two centuries is inconclusive, it is easier to assume that infants were baptized from the apostolic era than it is to explain why they were not. By the time infant baptisms clearly enter the record, they appear as nothing new. The first Christians probably baptized infants as naturally as they bathed, clothed, and fed them. The doctrine of original sin kept the practice from ever departing the Catholic tradition.

Stories of adult baptisms appear in Acts of the Apostles. Those who believed in Christ and sought participation in the Christian community could be baptized. The preparation for baptism expanded from charismatic preaching into the catechumenate. Even after infant baptism became the norm, the sacrament was always open to adults.

The age of confirmation has fluctuated considerably. From its origins one version of this sacrament could be celebrated with baptism. In that case, the age of confirmation has simply been the age of baptism. Infants and adults were confirmed at baptism at least through the thirteenth century, rarely by the fifteenth. But by the end of the twentieth century, adults, children of catechetical age, and infants in danger of death were confirmed at baptism.

However, another version of confirmation was celebrated on an occasion distinct from baptism, when the bishop offered it to those baptized by another minister. From the fifth through the thirteenth centuries, and rarely by the fifteenth, this group also included infants and adults. Beginning in the thirteenth century and quite commonly by the sixteenth, children could not be confirmed before age seven. However, extraordinary circumstances permitted their confirmation at a younger age. By the end of the twentieth century, seven remained the normal earliest age for confirmation, and many conferences of bishops were choosing late teenage years to increase a candidate's understanding and commitment. A significant number of people were probably never confirmed due to inconvenience.

So, the age for being anointed with chrism originally depended on the age of baptism. Then the occasion for confirmation shifted to the availability of the bishop (still requiring no minimum age of the candidate). Later it became associated with catechetical formation no earlier than age seven. In some places the age increased again to ascertain a more adult commitment from the candidate.

Although the sacrament of reconciliation was never considered an initiation rite, those baptized as infants were expected to celebrate it prior to the reception of the other sacraments. Penance was offered to those who had the capacity for sin and contrition; obviously, infants never celebrated this sacrament. From the thirteenth century the age of discretion was variously interpreted anywhere from seven to twelve or older. In the twentieth century it was set at about age seven.

The age for the first reception of Communion shifted from infancy to later years. The early Church offered Communion to infants, a practice that remained widespread until about the thirteenth century. Already beginning to wane in the preceding centuries, infant Communion disappeared rather quickly after the obligation for those at the age of discretion to receive Communion once a year came into force. By the thirteenth century the first reception of Communion was recommended for children ages ten to fourteen, although exceptions existed; infant Communion was forbidden. When the First Communion ceremony developed in the early seventeenth century, the participants were adolescents. The recommended age for First Communion reverted to seven in 1910 and remained there throughout the twentieth century.

In the history of the Western church, what was the sequence of confirmation and the first reception of Communion?

Table 1 shows the normal sequence of the sacraments and the reasons it shifted. In the two middle columns, a comma signifies separate occasions. A hyphen signifies the same occasion.

Table 1

CENTURY	NORMAL SEQUENCE	CANDIDATE AGE	REASONS
1–2	baptism, Communion	all ages	Gospel origins
3–4	anointing-baptism-Communion	all ages	Syrian practice
3–5	baptism-anointing-Communion	all ages	Western practice
5–13	baptism-Communion, confirmation	infancy, childhood	confirmation reserved to bishops
13–19	baptism, confirmation, Communion	infancy, 7, 10–14	First Communion delayed for discretion
20	baptism, Communion, confirmation	infancy, 7, 7–18	First Communion age lowered

Although the preceding chart attempts to show normal sequences, there were many exceptions and different sequential patterns coexisted. These patterns changed according to several factors, including the number of occasions on which the sacraments were celebrated, the age of the candidates, and the rank of the minister.

1. Two Occasions: Baptism, then Communion

Evidence from the New Testament and the early second century suggests that baptism was celebrated apart from Eucharist. The occasion for baptism was the conversion of the candidate. The first reception of Communion came on no special occasion with no notable ceremony. However, only the baptized were allowed to partake of Communion. New Testament records indicate that some of the baptized received an imposition of hands, but not an initiatory anointing; the evidence is not substantial enough to posit a consistent rite that entered into the pattern of initiation. If there is an "original" sequence of initiation rites, it is baptism, then Eucharist, on two separate occasions.

This pattern receded once the initiation rites began to be celebrated on a single occasion by the third century. However, it could have re-emerged between the third and the thirteenth centuries in extraordinary circumstances when, for example, a sick person was baptized by someone who was not a bishop where the Eucharist was not accessible, and then recovered to receive Eucharist on another occasion, but never was confirmed. Since the thirteenth century the pattern has been more common, since many people were never confirmed, even though they were baptized and received Communion at a later occasion. Obviously, these circumstances did not try to imitate the New Testament pattern, but happened due to sickness or inconvenience.

2. One Occasion: Handlaying/Anointing, Baptism, and Communion

By the second century, Syria had developed a single rite of initiation that included imposition of hands and anointing, followed by baptism and participation in the Eucharist. The pattern remained strong through the fourth century and may have endured in some cases into the sixth. Syria gradually added a post-baptismal anointing, so its sequence could resemble the conventional one in the rest of the Church. Once confirmation was established as an independent rite, this pattern never re-emerged in the Church.

3. One Occasion: Baptism, Handlaying/Anointing, and Communion—Bishop as Minister

By the third century infants and adults were initiated in a single ceremony, normally at Easter or Pentecost when the bishop was presiding, with baptism, an imposition of hands and/or an anointing, and Eucharist. Catechesis preceded for adults; some parents deferred the complete initiation of their children until they received some catechesis and life experience. Although this sequence gained almost universal acceptance from the third to the fifth centuries, it began to decline by the sixth, due to the large numbers of infants being baptized by presbyters. By the thirteenth century, the ritual still existed as a text, but it was rarely performed. It reappeared at cathedrals in the late twentieth century for the initiation of adults and children of catechetical age.

4. Two Occasions: Baptism and Confirmation, then Communion

Some people celebrated confirmation at baptism and then received Communion on a later occasion. A handlaying accompanies the twelve baptisms by Paul in Acts 19 (one assumes they partook of the Eucharist later), but it would be anachronistic to call it confirmation, and speculative to call it universal. This pattern is more clearly attested in the British Isles from the thirteenth to the fifteenth centuries, where bishops could confirm newly baptized infants, but their Communion was postponed. Elsewhere since about the thirteenth century the confirmation of infants by bishops was restricted to extraordinary circumstances, such as danger of death; in 1946 presbyters received permission to confirm the infants they baptized in danger of death; in both cases, infants who recovered received Communion at a later occasion.

5. One Occasion: Baptism

In some cases only baptism was administered. From the third century the Church defended the baptism of those near death, even without the other rituals. By the thirteenth century both confirmation and Communion had split from baptism; infants received baptism without the other rites, unless a bishop was present to confirm. Some never received confirmation or Communion due to death or neglect.

6. One Occasion: Baptism and Communion

Roughly between the fifth and the thirteenth centuries, when presbyters led most of the baptisms of infants, they offered Communion at the same time, though confirmation was deferred. Prior to the fifth century, some infants baptized in extraordinary circumstances could have followed this sequence. For the same reasons—death or neglect—some never received confirmation. After the thirteenth century the Communion of infants began to disappear and even became forbidden; it is conceivable that this sequence applied to some adults in independent instances.

7. Two Occasions: Baptism and Communion, then Confirmation

This sequence appeared at least by the third century when infants or adults in extraordinary circumstances were baptized without the presence of a bishop; if Communion was available, they probably received it. If they recovered, or if they later gained access to a bishop, he would have administered handlaying and/or anointing, even before the ceremony was called confirmation. Between the fifth and the thirteenth centuries, ministers offered Communion to newly baptized infants and adults; they were confirmed later when the bishop was available. For a time in the Carolingian era, this sequence proved popular even when a bishop was available for baptism. Between the thirteenth and the late twentieth centuries the pattern continued rarely, only when adult candidates for baptism may have been offered Communion when no bishop was present—presuming the baptized received confirmation later. Although canon law obliged twentieth-century presbyters to confirm children of catechetical age whom they baptized, many did not; they offered Communion and deferred confirmation until the bishop confirmed the children who had been baptized as infants.

8. One Occasion: Baptism, Confirmation, Communion— Presbyter as Minister

Persistently the Church exercised another option, the celebration of all the initiation rites with a presbyter, not with a bishop. Many Eastern rites have maintained this tradition consistently throughout their history. From the early fifth century in the West, when presbyters baptized, some of them anointed as well—with or without permission. Although Rome tried to eliminate the practice, evidence for it reappeared in the sixth and seventh centuries in Spain, Portugal, and the British Isles. In the Carolingian era, Gaul, northern Italy, and the British Isles still showed traces of the practice, and chorbishops and presbyters alike had to be restricted from confirming into the tenth century. In the late twentieth century, presbyters received the faculty to confirm adults and children of catechetical age whom they baptized; they offered Communion at the same time.

9. Three Occasions: Baptism, then Communion, then Confirmation

Some may argue that this pattern appeared in the Acts of the Apostles, where Peter and John imposed hands on a group who had already been baptized; no mention is made of Eucharist, but one could assume the new Christians had already shared at the table. Again, it is anachronistic to call this handlaying confirmation and speculative to call it universal.

One can more easily envision this sequence from at least the third century in emergency situations where baptism was administered to a sick person who recovered, gained access to Communion, but only later to confirmation. The sequence became more common from the ninth century, when Communion began to drift from the baptismal rite. Since the occasion for confirmation depended on the availability of the bishop and not on its sequence with Communion, some received Communion before they had the opportunity to be confirmed. By the thirteenth century, Communion was commonly deferred from baptism, and it often preceded confirmation, even through the twentieth century; some places developed policies promoting this sequence as early as the nineteenth century.

10. Three Occasions: Baptism, then Confirmation, then Communion

This sequence could have existed from the third century in some emergency situations, but more widely after about the ninth century when Communion began to separate from infant baptism. It was possible that some baptized infants were presented to the bishop for confirmation earlier than they received Communion. By the thirteenth century, when Communion commonly moved to ages ten to twelve, this sequence would have been very normal as confirmation was recommended not before age seven. It began to enter Church policies in the thirteenth to fifteenth centuries, probably as a way of encouraging people to be confirmed. Policies also developed from the seventeenth through the nineteenth centuries and remained customary in many locations through the twentieth. In early-twentieth-century Spain and Latin America, bishops often confirmed infants, and some priests in missionary countries were appointed to do the same.

11. Two Occasions: Baptism, then Confirmation and Communion

One can imagine this sequence under some emergency situations in the early Church. It was possible for a baptized sick person to recover and be presented to the bishop for confirmation and Communion. This was probably more common before the fifth century; once presbyters generally baptized, a recovering sick person would probably have had access to Communion before confirmation. Bucer introduced this practice during the Protestant Reformation. In the late twentieth century some communities favored the celebration of First Communion at a confirmation ceremony for those who were baptized as infants. Such rituals strove to imitate the early conventional sequence of the reception of these sacraments, even though this particular arrangement on two separate occasions was rare.

12. One Occasion: Baptism and Confirmation

Between the third and the ninth centuries, Communion was quite common at baptism, so if confirmation was given at the baptism, Communion must have been offered as well. Even between the ninth and the twelfth centuries, as the baptismal Eucharist fell into disuse, it would be hard to imagine a baptizing bishop offering confirmation but not Eucharist. After the thirteenth century, as the age for confirmation settled around seven, the confirmation of younger children was still permitted in extraordinary circumstances, but only between the thirteenth and the fifteenth centuries were bishops instructed to withhold Communion from infants they confirmed because of their age. Such children were candidates for this sequence if they died before receiving Communion or neglected it throughout their lives. Theoretically, throughout this period and up to the twentieth century, a bishop could baptize and confirm a young child in danger of death, who could have died without Communion. In the twentieth century, presbyters received permission to confirm infants they baptized in danger of death, so this sequence became much more possible.

13. Two Occasions: Baptism, then Confirmation

This sequence could have appeared any time after the ninth century when the baptismal Eucharist began to wane, in cases where someone who was baptized as an infant received confirmation at a later occasion, but through death or neglect never received the Eucharist.

14. Two or Three Occasions: Eucharist First

Clearly an anomaly, there are and have been occasions when people received the Eucharist before baptism. Even the legislation from the early Church reserving Eucharist to the baptized may have been addressing this situation. Some have done so in innocence, unbaptized visitors to the Christian assembly helping themselves to Communion. Others have responded to an invitation to open Communion erroneously proclaimed by a presiding minister.

The history of the initiation sacraments is rife with variations in sequence; furthermore, many co-existed.

Reconciliation in Sequence

Adding the sacrament of reconciliation would modify these sequences. Although reconciliation has never been called a sacrament of initiation, it is a sacrament that the Church has located within the sequence of other rites, which now are called initiatory. If deferred confirmation and Communion are still "initiation," one could argue that reconciliation that precedes them is a sacrament of initiation as well, since it is a sacrament celebrated within the period of initiation. In fact, it would not be surprising for a typical Catholic to name baptism, reconciliation, and First Communion incorrectly as the sacraments of initiation.

The confession of sins has taken different positions in the sequence of sacraments. It became part of the preparation for Communion in general by the late Middle Ages, and part of preparation for First Communion from the thirteenth century, but especially by the sixteenth. Since the sequence of confirmation and First Communion at that time depended solely on the availability of the bishop, possible four-stage sequences included baptism-confirmation-penance-Communion, baptism-penance-confirmation-Communion, baptism-penance-Communion-confirmation, and even a five-stage sequence: baptism-penance-confirmation-penance-Communion or baptism-penance-Communion-penance-confirmation. This five-stage pattern is actually implied by the *Catechism of the Catholic Church*. Of course, since death or neglect interrupted the celebration of confirmation or Communion or both, the number of possible sequences continues to multiply.

Reconciliation, a sacrament the Church expects to be celebrated within the years ascribed to sacraments of initiation, makes it even more difficult to unify the history of the sequence of these sacraments.

Baptism/Initiation Issues

By establishing two separate initiation patterns, one for infants and one for adults, the Catholic Church left unresolved the relationship of baptism and initiation.

Since some receive three sacraments at their baptism and others only one, one could surmise that there are different levels of initiation and membership. One who has received only one or two of the sacraments does not share the privileges of those who have had all three. For example, canon law restricts membership in religious orders, candidacy for priesthood, and nominees for godparents to those who have received baptism, confirmation, and Eucharist. By implication, others have a lesser status. Sometimes that status is freely chosen, for example when an adolescent receiving Communion refuses to be confirmed. An anomaly to the Eastern traditions, this situation results when confirmation is popularly interpreted as a self-appropriation of faith.

Furthermore, baptism is regarded not just as the gateway to the other sacraments but as participation in the life of Christ. Even though Jesus himself promised life only to those who were born again and who feasted on his body and blood, the Church's practice assumes that life in Christ does not depend on receiving Communion, much less on confirmation. So baptism alone imparts a complete participation in a heavenly reality, but a partial participation in an ecclesial reality. In one sense, it marks a complete initiation; in the other, it does not.

Another way to frame these sacraments is to ask if "initiation" really is the proper descriptor for them when they are spread out over so many different years and occasions. The expression "sacraments of initiation" is of late-twentieth-century vintage. The Church, which kept confirmation and Communion separate from baptism over so many centuries, never called them "initiation rites" until after Vatican II. Was this innovative description of the council accurate?

An alternate category for some of these rituals could have been sacraments "of discretion," or "of the use of reason." Confirmation (except in emergencies), reconciliation, Communion, and anointing of the sick are reserved for those who possess the capacity for catechetical formation, learning, and judgment. Orders and marriage require even more maturity. Perhaps "initiation" is less expressive for a category of sacrament that supplies rites for the attainment of a certain development in human life.

Even though the council restored the single occasion baptism-confirmation-Communion model to the adult catechumenate, it never did identify it as the single paradigm for all initiation. If the Church had described that unit alone as "sacraments of initiation," it would have more clearly assigned value to one sound ritual vision by asserting in a new historical period the priority of one initiatory model. This would have been significant because, as this history has shown, the Church has tolerated many different models of sequence, occasion, and ages of initiation. For its normative model of the catechumenate, the council chose not the oldest one, nor the one with the most common usage. It prudently chose one that expressed a coherent theology of initiation, which has exercised influence over the celebration and interpretation of the rites throughout history. In choosing that model for the Christian initiation of adults, the council boldly disabled the great disintegration of the initiation rites over the centuries in the West. But the Church has implied that the celebration of these sacraments on separate occasions still represents the same model, since the sacraments are identical. However, the more strongly one upholds the single occasion baptism-confirmation-Communion model, the more one realizes that the celebration of these sacraments over a period of years is just not the same model, even if it follows the same sequence.

The ambiguity surrounding the meaning of the expression "sacraments of initiation" permits perceived levels of Church membership, fails quite to name a stage of the Christian life, and leaves dubious the Church's commitment to a normative model.

Confirmation Issues

The meaning of confirmation has become obscure due to the increase in occasions for its reception, ages of the candidates, and ministers who confer it. Not uncommonly, a typical Catholic will describe confirmation as a rite of personal commitment to faith. Ironically, it has become in popular Catholic piety what the Protestant Reformers made it to distinguish it from the Roman sacrament.

The variations have created mass confusion on confirmation.

The age for receiving confirmation remains a much debated topic. It is secondary, however, to a discussion on meaning and occasion. If confirmation means a rite of commitment, its occasion should be distinct from infant baptism and the candidates' ages should reflect their maturity. But if confirmation is a rite of initiation, its occasion should be baptism and the candidates' ages should be determined by baptism alone.

The sequence of confirmation with Communion will depend upon its meaning as well. If confirmation is a sacrament of commitment, the only argument for placing it before Communion is that Communion should require commitment as well; without that sequence, confirmation lessens the commitment inherent in receiving Communion. However, if confirmation is an initiation rite, if it consecrates the baptized, it should precede Communion.

The proper minister of confirmation has changed considerably, especially in the last century. The more presbyters receive permission to confirm, the more difficult it becomes to see why this sacrament should be displaced from baptism at all.

A real pastoral problem surfaces in many parishes at Easter. Sometimes an unbaptized child of catechetical age has entered the catechumenate at an age younger than the diocesan age for confirmation. When that child is confirmed, parents of children baptized as infants do not understand why their children must wait for confirmation. The reason is the Church applies different standards for candidates based on their age at baptism.

The Church recommends confirmation before marriage, and some dioceses require it. For some engaged couples the preparation for these two sacraments becomes intertwined. Strangely this practice associates confirmation more with marriage than with baptism.

Other problems arise. People wonder what happened to the slap, why the ritual no longer recommends taking a name, why the sponsor should be a baptismal godparent, and why policies differ not just from one country to another, but from one diocese to another, literally across the river or across the street. These questions persist because the Church has inherited a sacrament too diverse in its application to catechize effectively about its meaning.

Confirmation has suffered variations since the Church made accommodations for emergency baptisms as far back as the third century. Its problems are older than its name.

First Communion Issues

The First Communion ceremony came into popular usage as a grassroots movement. Although Rome has indicated support for its existence, there is no universal rite of First Communion; the celebration has been handed down by personal testimony. The ceremony was constructed to instill a memory and inspire devotion in the children who received and the adults who witnessed. Parochial efforts to adjust First Communion traditions frequently meet resistance because to change is to threaten the very component that gave guidance to the ceremony: memory. Consequently, the ceremony has witnessed very few alterations even though the age of the recipients changed after 1910 and the theology of Eucharist and the sacraments of initiation changed after 1965.

Several issues come to light: eligibility for First Communion, the theological significance of its sequence with confirmation, and the perception of First Communion as a rite of initiation.

Eligibility for the Eucharist in the early Church was based on a simple criterion: the first and most basic prerequisite ever developed for participation in the Eucharist was baptism. It required no additional demonstration of personal readiness; baptism into the communion of Christ merited participation in the communion of Christ. Naturally, since infants were being baptized, infant Communion developed in East and West almost completely unchallenged. It has endured in the East, and it lasted over a thousand years in the West.

By the thirteenth century, the West looked for three additional criteria: discretion, the use of reason, and reverence. Children needed to show responsible moral behavior, an understanding of the difference between eucharistic food and ordinary bread, and spiritual devotion to the Eucharist. These criteria, added to baptism, removed eligibility for the Eucharist from infants.

The exclusion of children from the Eucharist indicates that Communion has more to do with behavior and formation than with baptism. Even so, children still perceive instinctively the original insight of baptismal Communion: it signals belonging. Before First Communion, children feel left out at the eucharistic table; after, they feel like they belong. Canonically, the youngest members of the community surprisingly join ranks with the excommunicated, apostates, heretics, and serious offenders—baptized Christians all who may not receive Eucharist.

First Communion also raises the question of its sequence with confirmation. Although the history of the sequence of these two sacraments in the West reveals an immense laxity founded on practical solutions and theological disinterest, interest has increased considerably due to the implications of a wide-ranging age for confirmation. Vatican II called for a closer association of the initiation rites, but it did not explain the significance of their sequence. Practically speaking, it remains as impossible today as it ever was in history to guarantee when bishops would be available for confirmations throughout the Catholic world. So even though the East includes in its theology of chrismation the consecration of the baptized in preparation for the Eucharist, the West could never sustain that interpretation since it could not guarantee that sequence. Although individual dioceses and conferences of bishops promote one sequence over the other, no universal solution has emerged. This leaves First Communion with a mixed interpretation. It is a sacrament for which one does not have to be confirmed, and when confirmation is interpreted as the sacrament of commitment, Communion oddly may require reason and discretion, but not necessarily a commitment to Christ.

Furthermore, in the wake of Vatican II's insight that there are three sacraments of initiation, one should expect First Communion customs to reflect that belief. However, the ritual developed at a time when the Church had no awareness of the rite as initiation. The council did not request that the ritual be revised in the same way as confirmation, because there never has been a universal First Communion ritual to revise. To allude to initiation, the confirmation rite created a centerpiece of the renewal of baptismal promises and recommended the return of baptismal godparents for the role of sponsor. But First Communion rituals have made little conscious effort to link the experience to baptism and confirmation.

To be sure, First Communion has ecclesial significance. It establishes a new relationship between the children and the Church. By analogy it "initiates" children to the eucharistic table, though they have already been initiated to the Christian life.

Fundamentally, however, First Communion rituals exhibit a self-concept not of initiation or even of communion with God and the Church, but of attainment of a catechetical level and of privatized devotion to the Eucharist.

For example, the ritual is usually celebrated at about age seven after a course of study. In many places children prepare as a class and celebrate First Communion as a class at a special ceremony apart from the Sunday liturgy, attended by family and friends but not by the parish at large. Some families become very involved before First Communion—children and parents attending the required sessions—but become less involved later.

Others successfully stress the family as the catechetical unit by placing primary catechesis in the home and setting the celebration for a time when families can gather. Nevertheless, the preparation and ritual still highlight the attainment of some level of maturity. The child even receives a certificate. First Communion ceremonies tend to bring out complete families, even when they represent different faiths, when divorce and remarriage have separated and blended family units, and when some Catholic members do not regularly attend church or receive Communion. Families recognize the event as a significant rite of passage that unites them all even if it neutralizes the faith and practice of individual members.

Nor does the First Communion dress contribute to initiatory symbolism. Some have argued that the dress is baptismal in origin, but this does not fit the creation of the ceremony or the variation in the color of the boys' clothing. The veil and dress of girls, reminiscent of a bridal gown, has led to interpretations of participating in the Eucharist as in the eschatological wedding banquet; if so, it made more sense when the participants were adolescents and when Communion was infrequent. Some early witnesses call the outfit the dress of angels—probably angels who adore the real presence of God, not who receive Communion. If nothing else, the dress seems to represent formality in its origin and tradition ever since. It symbolizes First Communion, not baptism. The dress does not effectively connect the sacrament with initiation.

Photography has increased at First Communion ceremonies. Families come equipped to document the event with several different cameras from multiple angles, some still, some video. If First Communion takes place in a class, the class photo may mean more to children than the photo of the actual event. Photography highlights the achievement of both individual and class while it intrudes on the liturgical ceremony, distracting worshipers, exalting the role of media, and turning designated family members into reporters.

After the ceremony, children are frequently treated to a party. This gathering highlights the family unit once again, and affords the children an opportunity to receive gifts. The nature of the gifts also instructs about the self-concept of First Communion ceremonies. Children may receive rosaries, prayer books, books on lives of the saints, bibles, statues, and even missals—significant parts of Catholic Church life, but tokens of a privatized piety, which signal that Communion is a devotional exercise, not initiatory, not communal. Some children prefer to get money anyway, an indication that societal values permeate religious ritual. The party and gifts come only once; people do not commonly celebrate a First Communion anniversary. First Communion has more to do with leaving the past behind than with entering a relationship that naturally invites renewal—like weddings, ordinations, professions in religious life, and Easter baptisms.

Deferring First Communion some years after infant baptism has created a practice that tries to offset the liminal status of children between rituals. In some parishes, such children present themselves at Communion with their families to receive a blessing from the Communion minister. Some say the children feel more included; others say it only reinforces their exclusion. In either case, the equation of blessing with Communion indicates a lost sense of the sacrament.

Hence, the First Communion rite, although it is called a sacrament of initiation, still resembles what it was created to be: a celebration of eligibility for Communion, based on knowledge, behavior, and piety, pertaining more to human development than to baptism, confirmation, and the faith community. Besides, the entire custom sidesteps an insight of the early Church that Jesus apparently invited all the faithful equally to baptism and to Eucharist (cf. John 3:5 and 6:53).

Solutions

Most frequently the solution to these pastoral predicaments lies in the hands of those who can deal with them only partially. Those who formulate sacramental policies are left with the dilemma that whether Communion precedes or follows confirmation, and whether the age of the recipient is young or old, they can find some historical support for the decisions they make, but history alone does not resolve all the conflicting pastoral circumstances. History will need the support of theology and a sensible pastoral practice. Celebrating confirmation with or before First Communion is a sound solution easily within the grasp of ecclesial governing bodies. But the Church needs more.

The most comprehensive resolution to the issues surrounding initiation is for the West to restore full initiation at one ceremony to all candidates, regardless of age, including infants. The East has followed this practice since the days of the early Church. The West advanced a reform of adult initiation through the work of Vatican II, but the council did not adequately address the needs surrounding the initiation of children.

This solution would significantly change the minister of confirmation and the age of First Communion.

The ministry of confirmation should be entrusted to presbyters. Some presbyters naturally assumed this ministry, with or without permission, in almost every age of history in the West. The twentieth century has permitted the practice under more circumstances than ever before. Assigning presbyters the faculty to confirm at baptism would be a logical next step; this actually remains faithful to several traditions in the Church. It would also minimize the great numbers of unconfirmed Catholics, a problem caused by the inaccessibility of the minister. However, in some places even presbyters are in short supply and catechists baptize more regularly. Under such circumstances, the Church could simply dispense with confirmation, not requiring it for any further ecclesial service. If baptismal initiation suffices for eternal life, surely it could suffice for participation in the Eucharist, the celebration of Christian marriage, and service as a godparent or in religious life.

The Communion of infants has a long pedigree in the Church, both East and West. The restoration of Communion to the youngest members would affirm the implications of their baptism, remain faithful to the original requirements for participation in the Eucharist, respond to the gospel invitation, and emphasize that Communion is an expression of the community—its faith in the presence of Christ under the form of bread and wine, and its self-identity as the body of Christ.

History shows that sacramental practice in the West has meandered before and since the disintegration of the initiation rites. With restored rites for infants, it is still possible to bring unity and definition to the ages of initiation.

How to Use the CD-ROM

The accompanying CD-ROM provides further references and source documents to the ideas outlined in this summary book. Each subhead in this book is listed in "Chapter Overview" sections at the beginning of the corresponding chapters on the CD. The points in the overview section are linked to more thorough and expanded explanations of the ideas introduced in this summary book. The CD consists of fully linked HTML files of each individual chapter of the book, as well as a table of contents and an extensive bibliography.

To begin using the CD, simply open the file "contents.htm" in any HTML editing program, Internet browser (such as Netscape Navigator or Microsoft Internet Explorer), or compatible word processing program (such as WordPerfect 8.0 or higher, Microsoft Word 97 or higher, Microsoft Word 98 for Macintosh or higher).